T0080689

Scorpion
vs.
Tarantula

Isabel Thomas

capstone

Heinemann Read and Learn are published by Heinemann,
1710 Roe Crest Drive, North Mankato, Minnesota 56003
www.mycapstone.com

Library of Congress Cataloging-in-Publication data is available on the Library of Congress website.

ISBN 978-1-4846-4070-8 (library binding)
ISBN 978-1-4846-4074-6 (paperback)
ISBN 978-1-4846-4078-4 (ebook pdf)

Edited by Penny McLoughlin
Designed by Steve Mead
Picture research by Svetlana Zhurkin
Production by Katy LaVigne
Originated by Capstone Global Library Limited

Acknowledgements
We would like to thank the following for permission to reproduce photographs: Dreamstime: Dmitrijs Mihejevs, cover (right); Getty Images: James H Robinson, 13, 17, 22 (top left), Tom McHugh, 11; iStockphoto: Kwanchai6632, 10; Minden Pictures: David Shale, 14, Stephen Dalton, 18; Shutterstock: amyai, 6, AppStock, 7, Audrey Snider-Bell, back cover (right), 5, 20, B & T Media Group, 19, efendy, back cover (left), 8, 22 (middle left), fivespots, 7 (tarantula silhouette), 22 (top right), frank60, 21, 22 (bottom left), GTS Productions, 12, just_yulianna, 4 (wood chips), Milan Vachal, 22 (bottom right), nale (man silhouette), 6, 7, ottmaasikas, 15, Pairoj Sroyngern, 6 (scorpion silhouette), pashabo (texture), cover and throughout, Popumon, 16, 22 (middle right), Ryan M. Bolton, 9, UpPiJ, cover (sand), wisawa222, 4 (scorpion), yod67, cover (left)

Every effort has been made to contact copyright holders of material reproduced in this book. Any omissions will be rectified in subsequent printings if notice is given to the publisher.

Some words are shown in bold, **like this**.
You can find them in the glossary on page 22.

Table of Contents

Meet the Animals

What has **pincers** and a sharp tail? It's the **Emperor scorpion**.

4

What has eight legs and a hairy body?

It's the
Goliath tarantula.

Would a scorpion or a tarantula win in a fight?
Let's find out!

Size and Strength

If an Emperor scorpion sat on your arm, it would reach from your hand to your elbow. A scorpion's front legs are big to help it catch prey.

This is how big an Emperor scorpion is next to a human.

This is how big a Goliath tarantula is next to a human.

Even an Emperor scorpion is small next to a Goliath tarantula! A Goliath tarantula is big enough to drag a baby bird out of its nest.

Speed

A scorpion **scuttles** quickly when it's striking at prey or trying to escape danger. A scorpion's front legs can crush an insect easily and give bigger animals a nasty nip.

A tarantula usually moves very slowly.
But it bursts into a run when chasing prey.
A tarantula doesn't need to spin webs.
It uses its strength to pounce on prey.

Defense

If there is nowhere to hide, a scorpion will stay as still as possible. Some fall into a deep sleep, as if they have been frightened to death.

A tarantula has hard skin. To let its body grow, a tarantula wriggles out of its old skin. Its body is soft and weak afterwards until the new skin hardens.

Survival Skills

A scorpion is an incredible survivor. It can live without eating for a year. It can even be frozen in ice and walk away unhurt after!

A tarantula likes to catch one meal every week in summer. Food is harder to catch in winter, so many tarantulas sleep through the winter in **burrows**.

Super Senses

A scorpion has bad eyesight. Instead, its legs and **pincers** are covered in many small hairs. A scorpion uses these to sense movement.

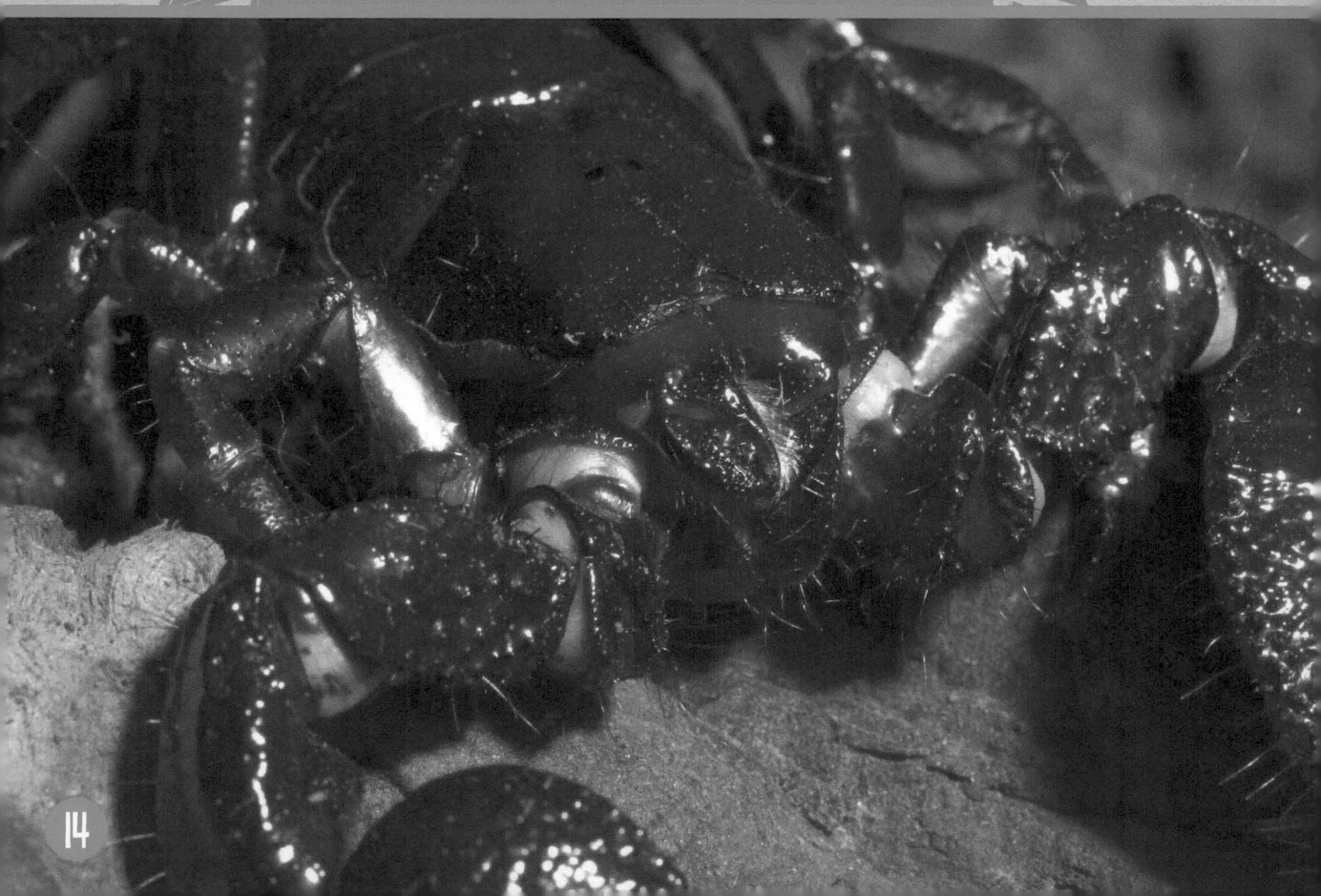

A tarantula's body is designed to blend in. This lets it hide from enemies. A tarantula the color of tree bark can sit on a tree without being spotted by hungry birds.

Deadly Weapons

A scorpion's **sting** contains some of the strongest **venom** in the world. A scorpion grips prey in its large **pincers** while it jabs its sting into the **victim's** body.

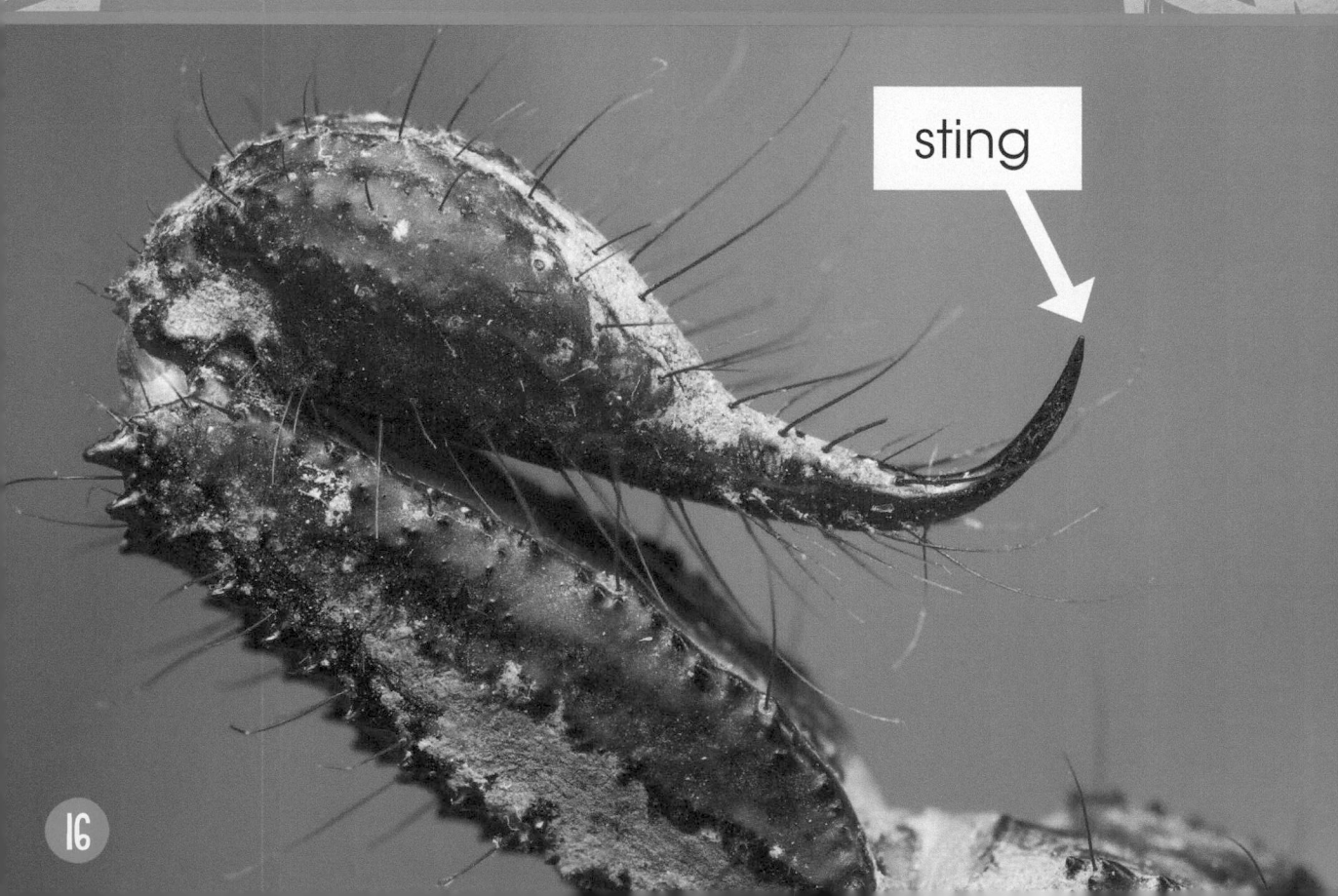

sting

fang

A tarantula has two huge fangs. These are strong enough to bite through human skin. Before an insect can attack with a sting or pincers, a tarantula tries to bite it.

Fighting Skills

With its **pincers** up and its **sting** pointed at the enemy, a scorpion will look terrifying. The **venom** in its tail can either kill an enemy or freeze it in its tracks.

A tarantula lifts its front legs up and shows its fangs to warn it is about to attack. It rubs its hairy legs together. This makes a loud hissing noise to frighten the enemy.

Who Wins?

What would happen if a scorpion faced off against a tarantula?

The tarantula would raise its front legs and hiss. The scorpion would flash its giant **pincers**.

But who would win?

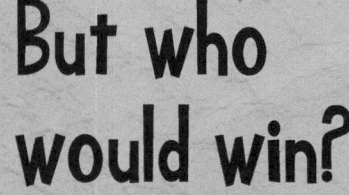

	Scorpion	Tarantula
Size	7	10
Strength	8	6
Speed	7	7
Energy	10	9
Skin	9	9
Senses	8	8
Venom	10	7
Weapons	10	6
Fighting skills	8	10
Attack	10	8
TOTAL	**87/100**	80/100

SCORPION WINS!

Picture Glossary

burrow—animal's hole in the ground

pincer—claw that can grip tightly

scuttle—move along with lots of short, fast steps

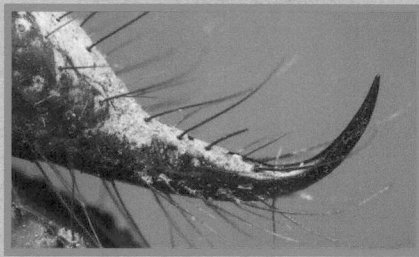

sting—part of an animal that can prick the skin and cause pain

venom—toxic liquid passed into a victim's body through a sting

victim—someone who is harmed by a bad event

Find Out More

Books

Bredeson, Carmen. *Tarantulas Up Close* (Zoom in on Animals!). New York, NY: Enslow Elementary, 2012.

Davin, Rose. *Scorpions* (Meet Desert Animals). Mankato, MN: Capstone Press, 2017.

Pallotta, Jerry. *Tarantula vs. Scorpion* (Who Would Win?). New York, NY: Scholastic, 2016.

Internet sites

Facthound offers a safe, fun way to find Internet sites related to this book. All of the sites on Facthound have been researched by our staff.

Here's all you do:

Visit www.facthound.com

Type in this code: 9781484640708

Index

by Chris Oxlade

capstone

To contact Capstone Global Library please call 800-747-4992, or visit our website www.mycapstone.com

Edited by Helen Cox Cannons
Designed by Philippa Jenkins
Picture research by Svetlana Zhurkin
Production by Steve Walker
Originated by Capstone Global Library Ltd

Library of Congress Cataloging-in-Publication Data
Library of Congress Cataloging-in-Publication data is available on the Library of Congress website.
ISBN 978 1 4846 4038 8 (hardback)
ISBN 978 1 4846 4042 5 (paperback)
ISBN 978 1 4846 4046 3 (eBook)

This book has been officially leveled by using the F&P Text Level Gradient™ Leveling System

Acknowledgments
We would like to thank the following for permission to reproduce photographs: Alamy: Sueddeutsche Zeitung Photo, 22; Dreamstime: Marilyn Gould, cover (left); iStockphoto: BernardAllum, 12; Library of Congress, 21; NASA, 25, 29; National Geographic Creative: H.M. Herget, 10; Newscom: akg-images, 17, 18, 19, 20, Design Pics, 8, Heritage Images/London Metropolitan Archives, 16, Heritage Images/Werner Forman Archive, 6, Hilary Jane Morgan, 11, Mirrorpix, 15, Mirrorpix/Arthur Sidey, 23, picture-alliance/dpa/ Andrej Sokolow, 28, Polaris/Solar Impulse/Rezo/Jean Revillard, 27, Universal Images Group/G. Dagli Orti/ De Agostini, 9, World History Archive, 13; Shutterstock: Everett Collection, 14, IM_photo, 5, Jeffrey B. Banke, 7, K_Boonnitrod, 4, Michael Shake, 1, Nerthuz, cover (right), Pavel L Photo and Video, 26, wws001, 24.

We would like to thank Matthew Anniss for his help in the preparation of this book.

Every effort has been made to contact copyright holders of any material reproduced in this book. Any omissions will be rectified in subsequent printings if notice is given to the publisher.

Table of Contents

Some words are shown in bold,
like this. You can find out what they
mean by looking in the glossary.

Thousands of years ago, during the Stone Age, most people in the world did not travel far from home. There were no cars or bicycles and no roads. People might have walked along a path to the next village.

People learned to train animals such as yaks to carry packs about 6,000 years ago.

Millions of people fly in airplanes every day.

Since the Stone Age, there have been many new inventions. They have made transportation easier and faster. We can now travel easily between towns and cities. We can even travel halfway around the world in a day in airplanes.

The wheel was invented in about 3500 BC. The first wheels were made of planks joined edge to edge. A simple two-wheeled cart could carry a lot more on it than an animal could carry on its back.

This work of art was made in 2500 BC. It shows Sumerians using a cart with an early version of wheels.

Cart wheels wore tracks into the stones of this Roman road.

Wheels with **spokes** were invented in about 2000 BC. Spoked wheels were lighter and stronger than solid wheels. Hundreds of years later, the ancient Romans began building roads paved with stone. This made travel across their huge **empire** easier.

People may have gone to sea on rafts made from logs or **reeds** as long as 40,000 years ago. The oldest boats ever found are from around 10,000 years ago. They were dugout canoes made out of tree trunks.

Dugout canoes were made by burning away wood to make a hollow.

Egyptian boats had sails made from **papyrus** or **linen**.

People simply paddled their boats until sails were invented in about 3100 BC. The first known sailing boats traveled on the River Nile in Egypt. Their square sails were raised up to catch the wind.

9

Trade and Discovery

Around the world, craftsmen slowly learned how to build bigger, stronger, and faster ships. Most ships had a **hull** of wooden planks over a wooden frame. **Cargo** such as **grain**, wine, and oil were loaded on board.

The ancient Greeks traded goods around their empire.

A **carrack** was a ship that sailed around Europe during the 14th century.

Explorers sailed across the oceans to explore new land. Some went to claim new land as their own. New inventions such as the **rudder** made long journeys by sea much easier.

Canals and Railroads

During the 1800s, engineers in Europe and the United States dug hundreds of miles of canals. Barges carried **cargo** such as coal or dry foods along the canals between cities, ports, and factories. A barge could carry more than a wagon on a road.

This illustration from 1828 shows barges carrying cargo along a London canal.

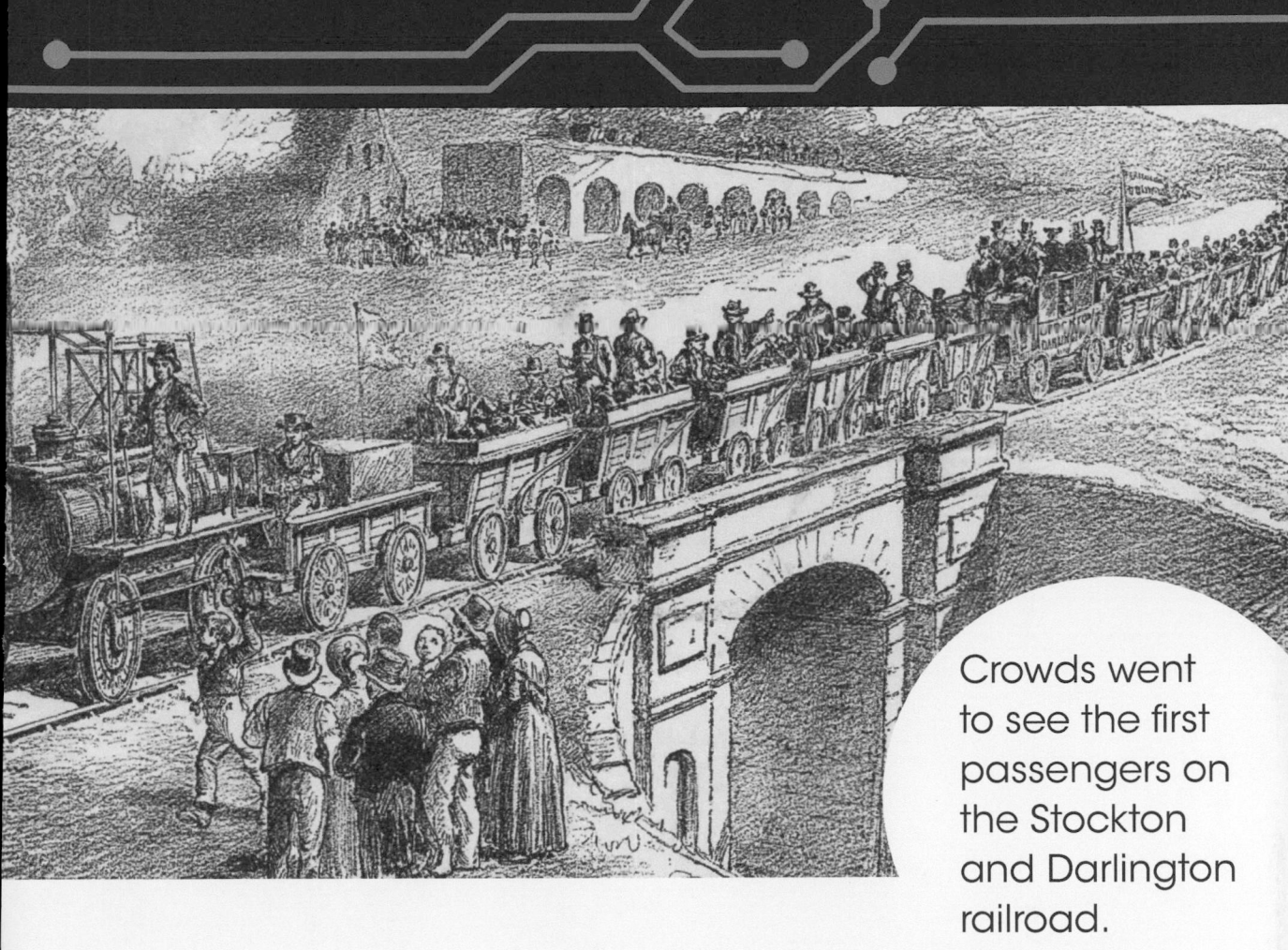

Crowds went to see the first passengers on the Stockton and Darlington railroad.

In 1825, the world's first passenger railroad started running. It was called the Stockton and Darlington Railway. Passenger coaches were pulled along by horses, then later by steam-powered **locomotives**. The first underground railroad opened in London in 1863.

Steamships

By the end of the 1700s, steam-powered ships began to take over from sailing ships. Steam engines turned paddle wheels or propellers in the water. Steamships were easily faster than sailing ships because they did not need wind to power them.

In 1819, *Savannah* became the first steamship to cross the Atlantic Ocean.

paddle wheel

French liner SS *Normandie* was the fastest liner of its time.

Shipbuilders began building steamships with metal instead of wood. By the 1930s, huge steam-powered liners were carrying people around the world. The biggest and fastest liners sailed across the Atlantic Ocean between Europe and the U.S.

In 1817, German engineer Karl Drais invented a heavy wooden bicycle with no pedals. It was known as a **draisienne**. In 1885, the first modern-looking bicycle was built. It was the Rover Safety bicycle.

A rider moved a **draisienne** along by pushing his or her feet against the ground.

Daimler's motorcycle was the first in the world.

In 1869, Frenchman Ernest Michaux put a small steam engine on a bicycle. Then, in 1885, Gottlieb Daimler built a motorcycle with a gas engine. Within a few years, motorcycles were popular across Europe and the U.S.

The word "car" possibly comes from the Romans. The Latin word *carrus* means "wheeled vehicle." The first cars of the 1800s were horse-drawn carriages with engines. German inventors Karl Benz and Gottlieb Daimler built two of the very first cars in 1885 and 1886.

Karl Benz built this car in 1885.

Ford built a special factory to build the Model T car.

Before long, there were lots of small car-making factories. But these cars were very expensive. Then, in 1908, the Ford Motor Company started making their Model T car. It was small, cheap, and easy to look after.

In 1783, a human took off in a flying machine for the first time. The machine was a hot air balloon. It was built in France by the Montgolfier brothers. About 100 years later, people began to travel in giant gas-filled airships.

Between 1928 and 1937, the Graf Zeppelin airship took thousands of people across the Atlantic Ocean.

Orville was the pilot of the *Flyer's* 12 second flight. Wilbur ran along beside it.

American brothers Orville and Wilbur Wright made history in 1903. They built the first successful powered airplane. It was called the *Flyer*. The *Flyer's* first flight lasted just 12 seconds. Many other inventors soon took to the air.

By the end of World War I (1914–1918), there were large bomber aircraft. Some of these bombers were turned into planes to carry passengers. These were the first airliners. Airliners got larger, faster, and more comfortable through the 1920s and 1930s.

The *Boeing 314 Clipper* was a flying boat that landed on water.

The giant *Boeing 747* airliner made its first flight in 1970.

The jet engine was a very important invention in the history of air transportation. It allowed aircraft to fly much faster and higher than before. The first jet fighter planes flew in 1939. By the 1950s, big jet airliners were taking off.

Rockets are machines that transport spacecraft into space. Rockets were developed in the 1920s and 1930s. By the 1960s, rockets were carrying astronauts onboard spacecraft into space.

Soviet **cosmonaut** Yuri Gagarin went into space in 1961, on board a Vostok spacecraft.

Armstrong and Aldrin landed on the moon in this lunar module.

In 1969, two American astronauts, Neil Armstrong and Buzz Aldrin, landed on the moon. They traveled there with Michael Collins in the *Apollo 11* spacecraft. Another spacecraft, the *Space Shuttle*, made dozens of trips to space between 1981 and 2011.

Types of fuel in engines include gasoline and **diesel**. These engines give out gases that **pollute** the air. In the 1990s, **hybrid** cars and electric cars were developed. Electric cars do not pollute the air.

Electric cars must be **recharged** when their batteries run down.

Solar Impulse 2 is a solar powered plane. It flew all the way around the world in 2016.

Engineers are now making solar powered cars, boats, and planes. This means they have solar panels that capture light from the sun. The vehicles then turn the light into electricity to power their electric motors.

What new forms of transportation will we see in the near future? Driverless cars are already being tested and driverless taxis are being used in Pittsburgh, Pennsylvania. The car drives itself. It finds its way from place to place by computer. We could all be using driverless cars one day.

This is a driverless car being tested by Google.

NASA is building a spacecraft called *Orion*. One day, it might carry people to Mars.

In the air, **drones** and giant airships may start carrying **cargo**. Engineers are designing new spacecraft. They hope these spacecraft will one day carry astronauts and all their food and equipment to Mars.

Glossary

cargo—goods carried on a ship or other vehicle

carrack—a medieval sailing ship with three or four masts

cosmonaut—a Russian astronaut

diesel—a type of fuel used in many vehicle engines

drone—an unmanned, remote-controlled aircraft

empire—a group of countries ruled by a single person or government

grain—wheat, or other type of cereal

hull—the main body of a ship, which makes it float

hybrid—a car that has both an electric motor and an engine that uses fuel

linen—a type of cloth similar to cotton

locomotive—railroad engine

papyrus—material made from papyrus, which is a water plant

pollute—to put harmful or dangerous chemicals into the environment

propeller—a device with spinning blades that help a ship or airplane move

recharge—to put electricity into a battery, so the battery can be used again

reed—a plant with tall leaves that grows in water or on wet ground

rudder—a flat handle at the back of a boat used for steering

spoke—a rod that joins the center of a wheel to the rim of a wheel

Read More

Davis, Lynn. *Henry Ford*. Amazing Inventors & Innovators. Minneapolis: Abdo Publishing, 2016.

Peterson, Megan Cooley. *The First Airplanes*. Famous Firsts. North Mankato, Minn.: Capstone Press, 2015

Simons, Lisa M. Bolt. *Transportation Long Ago and Today*. Long Ago and Today. North Mankato, Minn.: Capstone Press, 2015.

Internet Sites

FactHound offers a safe, fun way to find Internet sites related to this book. All of the sites on FactHound have been researched by our staff.

Here's all you do:

Visit *www.facthound.com*

Type in this code: 9781484640388

Index